Hysteria

Julia Borossa

Series editor: Ivan Ward

ICON BOOKS UK

TOTEM BOOKS USA

Published in the UK in 2001
by Icon Books Ltd., Grange Road,
Duxford, Cambridge CB2 4QF
E-mail: info@iconbooks.co.uk
www.iconbooks.co.uk

Published in the USA in 2001
by Totem Books
Inquiries to: Icon Books Ltd.,
Grange Road, Duxford
Cambridge CB2 4QF, UK

Sold in the UK, Europe, South Africa
and Asia by Faber and Faber Ltd.,
3 Queen Square, London WC1N 3AU
or their agents

Distributed to the trade in the USA
by National Book Network Inc.,
4720 Boston Way, Lanham,
Maryland 20706

Distributed in the UK, Europe,
South Africa and Asia by
Macmillan Distribution Ltd.,
Houndmills, Basingstoke RG21 6XS

Distributed in Canada by
Penguin Books Canada,
10 Alcorn Avenue, Suite 300,
Toronto, Ontario M4V 3B2

Published in Australia in 2001
by Allen & Unwin Pty. Ltd.,
PO Box 8500, 83 Alexander Street,
Crows Nest, NSW 2065

ISBN 1 84046 242 6

Series editor: Ivan Ward

Typesetting by Hands Fotoset

Printed and bound in the UK by
Cox & Wyman Ltd., Reading

Puzzles, definitions

'What is hysteria?' It might seem logical and methodologically sound to begin our investigation with this simple question. Unfortunately, it is precisely the question that has baffled, enraged or excited generations of physicians; inspired, infuriated or challenged priests, psychotherapists, artists and social commentators. The term 'hysteria' has been in circulation for over two thousand years. It is commonly assumed that Hippocrates, the 'father of medicine', first used it as a general descriptive term for ailments of the womb, but an identifiable disease entity corresponding to that term predates this usage by several centuries, recorded in Egyptian manuscripts. Nevertheless, consensus has not been reached as to whether hysteria still exists today or whether it has ever existed as such, let alone what it is.

Hysteria, as a descriptive category, has been applied in a variety of ways, across historical periods and cultural contexts. Puzzlingly, its referent has been simultaneously an illness with strange symptoms *and* certain disturbing forms of behaviour. Attempts to account for 'hysteria' have included pointing to a particular affliction which causes the womb to 'wander', to patients' propensity to lie and manipulate, to lesions of the nerves, to ecstatic states, to demonic possession, to forms of protest, to inexplicable epidemics. Artistic expression, seductiveness, wanting things in excess, behaving in a socially inappropriate way, partaking in crazes – all these have attracted the epithet 'hysterical'. Whether malady or maladjustment, the possibility of meaning many things in many ways runs through both usages of the term, which roughly correspond to the clinical and the common usages. Indeed, as we shall see, the two inform and shape one another. While the word 'hysteria' remains in current use, the formal diagnosis of hysteria, with its particular cluster of symptoms, or 'symptomatology', has largely ceased to be deployed in the course of the 20th century. However, the very symptoms that comprised hysteria have by no means disappeared, but are merely discussed and described elsewhere and otherwise.

As an illness, hysteria has had a long-standing association with the feminine. Although male sufferers were, at times, identified and discussed, it has primarily been seen as a woman's disorder. A key aspect of hysteria's manifestation was that it involved the sufferer's body, in a way that was changeable, and could not be put down to any tangible cause. Some of the classic symptoms of hysteria included: a feeling of suffocation, coughing, dramatic fits, paralysis of the limbs, and fainting spells, but also sudden inability to speak, loss of hearing, forgetting one's mother tongue, being proficient in languages that one did not know one knew, persistent vomiting and inability to take in food. In sum, it was a disease which appeared irrational, untrustworthy, and difficult to control.

The 19th century was the period of hysteria's heyday, and it was then that the metaphorical slippage between symptom and behaviour, the illness and its sufferers, came to the fore. Its direct effect was to unveil the location of hysteria within the realm of sexual politics. Within a predominantly patriarchal world-view, the hysteric came to embody femininity itself, as problem and enigma. This is the position from which Sigmund Freud approached her. The question, 'What does woman want?', which he famously posed in one of his late papers,[1] can be seen as a continuation of his fruitful confrontation with the puzzling illness he first studied as a young doctor. Indeed, it is no exaggeration to state that Freud's encounter with hysteria and the hysterical patient lies at the very origin of psychoanalysis. Among psychosomatic conditions, only hysteria, with its unique expressiveness and ability to symbolise conflict and distress in a kind of alternate language, would fit the bill and prove to be, along with dreams, 'the royal road to the unconscious'.[2]

From a standpoint critical of patriarchy – that is to say, from the standpoint of feminist theory and politics, or indeed from the standpoint of certain forms of artistic expression such as Surrealism – the hysteric has been seen as, alternatively, a victim (of oppressive social conditions) or a rebel (refusing those conditions) whose strange, disturbing behaviour expresses a sense of profound discomfort and/or protest towards the limitations of her – or his – situation. The question, 'What does woman want?', becomes then less a response to a clinical puzzle than a response to a political intervention. Whatever it is that she or he may want, it is not *this*.

Either way, hysteria picks up on a problematic, paradoxical relationship to conformity, played out primarily in the arena of the body: gendered, out of control and refusing an easy categorisation. But it is important to understand that hysteria is a reaction to certain aspects of human subjectivity, and as such it is not surprising that it is found trans-historically and cross-culturally. The fact that it is women who have most often been designated as the ones who bear and embody that reaction is itself a significant part of the issues highlighted by hysteria. As for psychoanalysis, an engagement with hysteria is not only present at its origins, but is bound up with the conceptual tenets which enabled its foundation as discipline and institution (the unconscious, transference, counter-transference, the complexity of sexuality). But psychoanalyst, beware: hysteria, like the unconscious itself, has a way of keeping its secrets.

A 'hystorical' approach

Tracing the idea of hysteria in psychoanalysis presents one with an unusual challenge. As the previous section has been suggesting, hysteria, although fundamental to the formation of psychoanalysis as both a particular form of therapy and a particular system of thought, brings with it its own chequered history. It has been necessary to unravel this history in some detail in order to show exactly what was at stake when Freud came to problematise human subjectivity and the therapeutic relationship. Psychoanalysis is, in some ways, the logical outcome of the questions that hysteria had been asking throughout the centuries about gender, conflict and power, and it provides its own way of putting them into narrative form, into its own case histories. So, in a way, the clinic of psychoanalysis takes over from the history of hysteria and forecloses it. It has been necessary here to retell the latter in order to illuminate the former.

Hysteria seems largely to disappear as a clinical diagnosis soon after psychoanalysis gets firmly established. Some of the psychic pain and conflict at the root of its symptomatology becomes enacted in other disturbances, such as eating disorders. Meanwhile, a whole separate clinical speciality, psychosomatic medicine, addresses itself to the question of how states of mind can cause physical symptoms to appear – minus, however, hysteria's complex symbolisations of conflict. While it would be incorrect to say that post-Freudian psycho-analysis ignored hysteria altogether,[3] nevertheless the problematics involved were first and most clearly expressed in those iconic texts of early psychoanalysis, *Studies in Hysteria* (1895) and 'Fragment of an Analysis of a Case of Hysteria' (1905). The point of a historical approach is not to present hysteria as fossilised and irrelevant to the contemporary world. Quite the opposite: the 19th century's hysteric enabled a certain Freudian con-ception of the human subject – as split, conflicted, sex-centred, alienated from itself – which is very much still with us at the inception of the 21st century. Hysteria continues to inform what it is to be human, and will no doubt continue to do so for some time into the Cyber Age. But let us now begin this investigation, this 'hystory', to borrow a pun from Elaine Showalter.

Mind, matter and behaviour

There is a standard way of following the trajectory of the story of hysteria across the centuries.[4] Most historians of medicine argue that something akin to hysteria existed in the ancient world. They identify elements that will accompany later conceptions of the condition: the connection with women's bodies, particularly their reproductive system, together with an added dimension which could be categorised as psychological – namely, dissatisfaction, particularly sexual dissatisfaction. The following passage from Plato's *Timaeus* captures well what was at stake.

The womb is an animal which longs to generate children. When it remains barren too long after puberty, it is distressed and sorely disturbed, and straying about in the body and cutting off the passages of breath, it impedes respiration and brings the sufferer into the extremest anguish and provokes all manner of diseases besides.[5]

Medical response included recommendations for increased sexual activity for the stricken patients.

The rise of Christianity with its emphasis on sinfulness, distrust of the flesh and woman's special guilt, provides the background to the next major twist in the tale. St Augustine's teachings were particularly influential in introducing conceptions of divine punishment into the understanding of disease in general, inasmuch as the afflicted subject was regarded as suffering the consequences of original sin. We cannot, of course, forget Eve's special role in that *débâcle*. In such a context, the hysteric, still almost exclusively a woman, was no longer perceived as having a condition that might be amenable to treatment, and while the sexual connotation of her symptoms remained part of the picture, it concentrated the condemnation and opprobrium upon her. The most common explanation of what was wrong with such women was that of possession by the devil; the figure of the witch was superimposed on that of the hysteric. Following suit, the most common response became a legal one involving the severest punishments – for example, burning at the stake.

Hysteria was re-medicalised from the 17th

century onwards, and with advances in anatomical knowledge, emphasis shifted away from the womb as the locus of the trouble, towards the brain and the nervous system. This shift allowed for a breach in the obvious link between hysteria and female anatomy, and indeed male sufferers began tentatively to appear in case accounts. But as the condition was no longer seen as depending on an exclusively female organ, a discursive link between hysterical character traits and femininity simultaneously came to the forefront. By the mid-19th century, hysteria was certainly perceived as an illness, but an illness inseparable from a certain way of behaving badly, one which was (and largely still is) perceived as feminine. While the core clinical picture – of changeable physical symptoms having no obvious organic root cause – remained in place, flirtatiousness, deceitfulness, exaggerated gestures, unseemly displays of emotion, excessive wants or dislikes, overt sexual behaviour or the ostentatious refusal of sex all became part of a proliferation of discourses, medical and popular, surrounding the hysteric. Talked and written about across Europe, hysteria would become the disease of the moment, coinciding with the profound changes which affected family structures under the pressure of industrialisation, particularly within an expanding middle class where the roles of men and women were polarised as never before, divided between the worlds of work and home.

Interrelated sets of concerns and practices regulated the way in which the strange illness and the troublesome patient were approached in the latter half of the 19th century. The first grouping involved theories of heredity and degeneration which were prevalent at the time. They had the effect of providing a scientific, biological justification of social divisions, and of vindicating social privilege which was no longer felt to be an innate, inheritable right in the new industrial bourgeois age. The reasons for a propensity for deviance from an ideal norm (a deviance that could manifest as madness, criminality, even physical weakness or sickliness) were thus to be found in one's family history. While not overtly culpable, the hysterical patient is nevertheless marked by her symptoms, locked into position as a suspicious pariah with a probably suspicious lineage. Although there certainly were well-to-do patients, class was now a prominent factor in the diagnosis of hysteria. This was all the more true in the case of men, who were heads of the family and responsible for handing down the family name.[6]

The second grouping involved the conception of the human being as split between a conscious, moral self, and something other, irrational, problematic, which needed to be reined in. The figure of the 'double', or *doppelganger*, so popular in 19th-century literature – Stevenson's *Dr Jekyll and Mr Hyde*, for example – is a representation of this idea, as is the Freudian conception of the *unconscious*, the foundation stone of psychoanalysis. Presenting a split or multiple personality began to feature prominently among the hysterical patients' irrational symptoms, and was explained as a marker of the tenuousness of their rational, controlling and in-control self.

The third grouping concerned the way in which human beings in their split nature were amenable to the influence of another. The relevance of this idea to therapeutics in particular was highlighted by the practice of magnetism or mesmerism, introduced in the 18th century by the Austrian physician Franz Anton Mesmer, who believed that good health, physical and psychic, was dependent on the free flow of a magnetic fluid which circulated within and between all things and all living beings. Disruptions in the flow could be corrected through a rapport between a patient (typically female) and a specially trained individual, the magnetist or mesmerist (typically male). Suspicions about the exact nature of this rapport, which had overt erotic overtones (knee-rubbing between magnetiser and magnetised, for instance), together with charges of charlatanism, contributed to the public disregard of Mesmer's theories, but his practice survived in several different countries throughout the 19th century. Usually known under the name of hypnotism, it allowed for the investigation of a range of irrational behaviours and phenomena, of which hysteria was most certainly one. It also, for some, held the promise of a potential treatment.[7]

Charcot and the spectacle of materiality

By the 1880s, the director of the Salpêtrière hospital in Paris, Jean Martin Charcot, and his followers, dominated the investigation of hysteria in Europe. Charcot's views were not without challengers, notably Hyppolite Bernheim, the leader of a rival school of thought based in the town of Nancy. As a young physician eager to perfect his training, Freud spent some time with both of these men, and the two contrasting takes on the condition of hysteria and the particular role of the doctor confronting it contributed the necessary backdrop to the insights that enabled Freud's elaboration of psychoanalysis.

When Charcot became fascinated by hysteria in the 1870s, he had already made his name studying a variety of neurological ailments. He began concentrating the resources of his hospital on the study of hysteria, with the stated aim of pinpointing its *materiality*. Instead of exploring ways in which body and mind influence one another, Charcot claimed outright that hysteria involved a particular *disturbance of the nervous system,* weakened by a *dodgy heredity.* Its onset, he argued, was often due to a *traumatic shock* such as an accident. It was therefore a physical occurrence, in contrast to the emotional occurrence that our own post-Freudian usage tends to associate with trauma. Charcot was a scientist with a liking for clear, tangible causal explanations. Nicknamed 'the Napoleon of neurosis', he could be more than a little overbearing. But he did have a genuine flair for showmanship and a well-developed sense of visual aesthetics. Freud called him 'a seer'. All these factors came into play in the work he did at the Salpêtrière.

Charcot had two ways of positively diagnosing and grounding hysteria. First, he sought to identify the patients' hereditary antecedents, which might be a contributing factor.

In the area of nervous pathology, there is no question of spontaneous generation and nothing ever comes from nowhere, it always has its pathological antecedents [. . .]. Heredity is interesting because it always brings us back to the same principle: it proves to us that hysteria does not grow all by itself, like a mushroom.[8]

Charcot also widely used hypnosis with patients who might be suffering from hysteria. According to his views, to be susceptible to hypnosis implied a predisposition to hysteria.

In a master stroke, Charcot imposed closure on the most flamboyant of the hysterical symptoms, the grand fit, by describing and documenting a regularity he perceived within it. He divided the fit into four phases, which he said recurred in every patient: (i) *période épileptoide*; (ii) *période de clownisme ou des grands mouvements* (contradictory, illogical phase); (iii) *attitudes passionnelles* (logical); (iv) *délire terminal*.

The object of Charcot's rigorous classifying system was precisely to rescue hysteria from the realm of the unknowable. His project involved a desire to tame the illness, and by extension, the hysterical patient, just as surely as if he had found the exact lesion in her nervous system which corresponded to every one of her symptoms (which of course he never did).

He then reinforced his classification of the fit by a vast visual apparatus of documentation. Diagrams, sketches, plaster casts, and above all hundreds of carefully labelled photographs functioned as a record of what went on at the Salpêtrière. In a series of particularly haunting images, a patient – the beautiful Augustine – smiles from her bed at an imaginary object of desire, at the photographer, at the audience, at us, with a stylised seductiveness familiar to us from the early days of silent cinema. The captions, though, penned by Charcot, fix what may be happening into his favoured narrative: *'Attitudes passionnelles . . . Phase 3'!*[9]

Charcot also presented his views to students – and as his fame increased, to visiting luminaries – in weekly lectures during which he 'demonstrated' the hysterical attack. A patient shared the stage with the master neurologist during his expositions. He would interview her and then hypnotise her to show off her susceptibility to attack. He would have his bevy of photogenic 'experts', eloquent and moving as they performed the expected hysterical attack. Some names remain on record: Augustine, Blanche Witman, Geneviève.

The hysteric could indeed speak – she was even heard – but still she was far from being listened to, for her expressiveness, her special kind of knowledge and experience, was mediated by the whole intricate Salpêtrière apparatus geared to the Charcotian representation of hysteria. At best, her expertise consisted in being the finest, most typical example of the already tamed disease. The hysteric did have stories to tell, but these – heard but not engaged with – constituted just more symptoms for Charcot to categorise. In a particularly poignant early case, Charcot described a hysteric whose attack consisted in reliving a series of frights she had had, over and over again. Her story certainly was heard, as it was recorded in the case, but it was marginalised in Charcot's telling. He considered it just another symptom, relegated to the sidelines. She, the teller, was reduced to pointless repetition, symptomatic hysterical babble. And the reliving, the telling of her tale, was repeated day after day, much as another hysteric's contraction or spasm, bringing her no relief.[10]

A famous painting by Brouillet captures the scene. Charcot is in mid-lecture, his expressive gestures and talk spellbinding a roomful of men assembled to hear him. Next to him, though, a woman is beginning to go into a hysterical attack. Her top has become undone as she falls backwards into the arms of an attendant preparing to catch her. This image, a copy of which hung over Freud's analytic couch and can still be seen at the Freud Museum in London, captures an eroticism which underlay the relationships at work in the vast 'museum of pathology' which the Salpêtrière had become.[11] Uneasily fitting into Charcot's quest for a sober neurological grounding to hysteria, yet permeating everything, this eroticism – theorised as transference and counter-transference – would find its rightful place at the centre of Freud's account of neurosis and of the doctor–patient relationship. It also unsettles power-relations which otherwise would seem to be operating so unambiguously in favour of Charcot and doctors in general, and raises the question of the role that the hysteric was playing. Object of desire? Subject of a scene of seduction? What you see is what you do not get. We shall turn to a fuller consideration of these issues later on.

The power of suggestion

But before we move on to consider the changes that psychoanalysis brought to the therapeutic relationship, we need to visit the clinical stage of Charcot's main rivals. The 'Nancy group' had a somewhat different way of dealing with hysteria. The group consisted of four men with differing professional backgrounds. The eldest, Ambroise Liébeault, a country doctor, was fascinated by older, quasi-obsolete mesmeric therapeutic traditions. He eventually gave up a conventional medical practice to devote himself to curing by hypnosis, and started drawing enormous crowds. Liébeault was joined by Hyppolite Bernheim, who became the actual leader of the Nancy school and wrote a series of well-regarded treatises on the condition. Jules Liégeois, a lawyer, and Etienne Beaunis, a forensic expert, completed the group, mainly studying the legal aspects of hypnosis and suggestion.

It was the *relationship* between hypnotiser and hypnotised, the influence of the former over the latter in the act of *suggestion*, which constituted the main interest of the Nancy group. Accordingly, their views on the hypnotic state were seemingly incompatible with the theories being promulgated at the Salpêtrière. Bernheim maintained that it was not a physical act which constituted the hypnotic factor, but a psychic process, an idea, generated by verbal suggestion. But what were the limits of the power exercised in that process? Could it be used for therapeutic purposes? Could it drive people to crime? While the latter question was of special interest to Liégeois and Beaunis, Bernheim, following Liébeault, explored the possibility of curing various nervous diseases through suggestion, diseases among which hysteria held a prominent place. The Nancy school, in its approach to hypnosis, was concentrating on the act of hypnotising and the rapport it established, rather than on the state itself and what could be achieved within it. Hysteria was interesting to them only inasmuch as it responded well to suggestion.

Moreover, suggestion itself was felt to be a universal state. For Bernheim, one of the bases of suggestibility was credulity, defined as 'the capacity to take things for granted, without needing proof'. Bernheim forcefully established this quality as one of the cornerstones of civilisation, without which there would be 'no education, no tradition, no history, no transactions, no social contract'.[12] To be sure, an opposition between the 'easily suggestible' and those who were made of sterner stuff was nevertheless maintained, a distinction which fed easily back into the existing social discourse about heredity and moral worth.

At the Salpêtrière, the erotic rapport between doctor and patient and its effect on the cure remained unacknowledged, or at least unstated, whereas the eroticism of the behaviour of many hysterics was unmistakable. The cure by suggestion, however, inherited from mesmerism itself the suspicious taint of sexual impropriety. Moreover, in most of the legal cases involving the criminal uses of suggestion, lovers were accused of exerting undue influence. A good example is the Chambige case, in which a young clerk was accused of hypnotising a respectable housewife and enticing her into a failed suicide pact, and which also served as an inspiration for the 1901 best-seller by Paul Bourget, *Le Disciple*. Other famous cases of the time involved actual murder sprees, and the newspapers became obsessed with the nature of criminal responsibility, particularly female guilt and innocence.[13] It is interesting to find parallels, and also differences, at work in the debates surrounding our own society's most notorious female criminals, such as Myra Hindley and Rosemary West. Were they under the unnatural influence of their men? The possibility, although ultimately widely rejected, has been raised in both of these cases.

But the Nancy school did not show any inclination towards theorising or even duly acknowledging these curious interminglings of eroticism, emotional ties and influence. This lack was quite typical. Pierre Janet was a psychologist who worked in Paris, but evolved his own approach to the treatment of nervous diseases, a method which combined the hysteric's recollection of trauma with the therapist's use of suggestion. He made the following observations in a study of hysterics suffering from *aboulia*, or loss of will. Seeing that several women were growing strongly attached to the attending therapist, he noted that:

The one who treats them is no longer in their eyes an ordinary man, he takes on an importance next to which nothing else counts.[14]

Janet then explicitly sought to distinguish what his patients felt for him from the '*passions magnétiques*' of old, which his critics were bound to bring up. He pointed out that there were many different varieties of that attachment, including perhaps erotic feelings but also fear and aversion, or even filial respect.

Only a superficial observer would give to such a passion a vulgar source and tie it to an erotic need.[15]

Janet and others seemed to treat this strange phenomenon in the same way as Charcot did hypnosis, considering it simply as a further symptom.

Untrustworthy patients: seen but not heard

Another important aspect of these various attitudes towards hysteria was that regarding malingering – in other words, the question of what credit, if any, one could attach to the hysteric's words. Malingering as a diagnosis or category tended to confuse two separate issues: that of the genuineness of the symptoms and that of the falsity of the patient's utterances. Charcot was generally regarded as a scientist who restored dignity and respectability to the hysteric, and this is partially true. In response to a widespread popular interpretation, connected to a mistrust of women deeply ingrained in the culture, which held that because hysterical symptoms had no physical basis they were deliberate lies, Charcot set out to prove the contrary. Thus, in some of his case studies he describes intricate mechanical contraptions which put the newest technology into the service of scientific truth. In one example, he uses a respiratory machine to measure the amount of effort a girl exerts in supporting a one-kilogram weight on her arm, which is contracted rigid and extended in a fit of hysteria. The control subject is a strong male assistant of Charcot who maintains through his conscious will a similar contraction. He soon huffs and puffs, while her breathing remains regular. The verdict is passed: she cannot be malingering.[16]

Yet, despite declaring the hysteric's symptoms to be genuine, it is clear that Charcot still regarded her utterances with great suspicion. A glance at the manner in which he interviewed his patients is also instructive. Always sure of the status of his own knowledge and mastery, he had a very clear notion of what he wanted to hear, as is obvious from the following dialogue taken from one of his case studies:

Charcot: *Do you vomit?*
Patient: *Continually.*
Ch: *You always exaggerate.*
[Charcot continues to question]
Patient: *Yes, because . . .*
Ch: *I do not ask you to give me theories. See how it is not always easy to interrogate patients. They always serve you up a quantity of spurious facts or interpretations that one cannot make any use of.*[17]

Similarly Liégeois, a lawyer by training, was especially prone to condemning the malingering hysteric, more so than his medical colleagues. He may have recognised the existence of her hallucinations, but his tone of moral condemnation is evident as he lists a series of famous cases where miscarriages of justice were carried out or only narrowly averted due to hysterics' false accusations, usually of a sexual nature.[18]

Both schools agreed to disregard what the hysteric actually *said*. This disregard was in the service of a quest to delimit clearly who actually was in control, doctor or patient, male or female. In the case quoted above, Charcot tellingly concludes in the following manner: 'One must know how to lead them through the right path of simple and disinterested observation.'[19] Similarly, in another case, he leads his patient to conform to his own theoretical model of the disease, the four stages of hysteria he had so carefully described. He had already identified from the patient's mother's description of the attack, phase two (*grands mouvements*) and phase three (*attitudes passionnelles*). He offers the mother a description of phase one, the *période épileptoide*, in the guise of a question: 'When she falls, before she bites herself and rolls around, is she not first of all stiff, for a moment, then given to shaking?' The mother answers, 'Yes, often, but not always'. Charcot is quick to declare that the cycle is complete.[20]

Essentially, the common attitude of all the therapists discussed in this section was to consider the patient's own version of her experience to be of little account. On the one hand, it was conceded that the malingering hysteric often could not help what she was doing because she had fallen prey to her own hallucinations. But a picture of the hysteric as malingerer continued to coexist with this more generous characterisation. Fundamentally, hysterics were not to be trusted, believed or listened to. In the end, despite the belief in the inevitable sway of heredity, or in the universal susceptibility of humans to suggestion and personal influence, a secure sense of their own place in the hierarchy of power was implicit in the clinical writing of these male practitioners.

Hysteria and the 'talking cure'

In sum, all the various views on hysteria we have been looking at had the effect of neglecting the question of the rapport between the hysteric and her doctor, even as that rapport was clearly at the very heart of their management and public presentation of the condition. They also persistently ignored, negated or misrepresented what the patient might have had to say about her condition, or, to phrase it slightly differently, what her condition, hysteria, might have been communicating through its mysterious somatic manifestations. Whether object of investigation or of treatment, the patient was indeed objectified by the prevalent scientific discourse.

This was about to change with the publication of *Studies in Hysteria* – a volume of case studies co-authored by Sigmund Freud and an older colleague, Josef Breuer – which represented the culmination of some ten years' reflection on hysteria. In this book, the two physicians argued three principal things: first, that the hysterics' symptoms made sense, inasmuch as they were the logical expression of a psychic (as opposed to a physical) trauma; second, that this trauma had to do with libidinal impulses which had been thwarted; and third, that a cure, of a cathartic nature, depended on the remembrance and expression of that trauma in narrative form, within the context of a therapeutic relationship. The 'talking cure' had been born.

The five women who figure in the book were allowed, indeed encouraged, to construct coherent stories of their illness, and beyond their illness, of their lives. The first case recorded Breuer's treatment of the woman he called Anna O. Her physical symptoms were as multiple and puzzling as any hysteric's. They included a seeming splitting of her personality, hallucinations, refusal to eat and various disturbances of the senses, including severe 'functional disorganisation of her speech', and periods of *aphasia* (the loss of ability to speak or express oneself). She would also spontaneously fall into a hypnotic state in the late afternoon, from which she would wake up and complain, uttering the words 'tormenting, tormenting' over and over. After a prolonged period of total inability to communicate, Breuer made a first crucial breakthrough by gaining an insight into the 'psychical mechanism of the disorder'. 'As I knew', he went on to write, 'she had felt very much offended over something and had determined not to speak about it. When I guessed this and obliged her to talk about it, the inhibition which had made any other kind of utterance impossible as well, disappeared'.[21] Breuer had made contact with Anna O.; he had assumed the position of her interlocutor, broken the isolation of her storytelling, and understood that her symptoms were *not random but made sense*. The deeply uncomfortable, barely contained erotic charge of Breuer's dialogue with Anna O. does not explicitly figure in the text of the case. It was only decades later, with an elaboration of transference and countertransference, that what really happened between doctor and patient became known. Anna O. apparently developed a phantom pregnancy and named Breuer as the father ('Now Dr. B.'s child is coming', she said).[22] Breuer terminated the treatment forthwith, and fled on a second honeymoon with his wife.

If the importance of narration within the context of a particular therapeutic relationship is the initial lesson to be drawn from this first case of 'talking cure', the second is the direct bearing on the narrative of scenes from the patient's past, the idea

that 'hysterics suffer mainly from reminiscences'.[23] Anna O.'s stories had as their starting
point a girl at a sickbed. As so many young women
of that period, she had devoted herself to nursing
her sick father. It was his death which changed the
course of her illness, precipitating the split in her
consciousness. Within this larger contextual structure, Breuer was able to connect her symptoms to
particular scenes in the past which had provoked
them. He found that:

*A number of extremely obstinate whims were [. . .]
removed after she had described the experiences
which had given rise to them.*[24]

These very same principles of narration and
reminiscence form part of the second case in
Studies in Hysteria, that of Frau Emmy von N.,
which was Freud's first full-length talking cure.
Her physical symptoms were manifold: various
pains, curious tics, and, as in the case of Anna
O.'s repetition of 'tormenting', a sudden, jarring
irruption of words. 'Keep still! Don't say anything!
Don't touch me!', were Frau Emmy's recurring

cries.[25] The method of treatment that Freud records himself as employing is largely one of straightforward symptom-elimination, through the dual method of first eliciting from the patient the stories which lie behind the symptoms, and then, through suggestion, eliminating the affective power of these memories. This afforded Frau Emmy some instant symptomatic relief, provided – and herein lay the lesson – that she had before-hand expressed all of the pathogenic connections surrounding one particular symptom–memory cluster. It is in this second case that the connection between the completeness of the narrative and the quality of the cure is made explicit. For example, two of her symptoms included stammering and clacking when she was afraid. She told of two major traumatic instances of fright in her past: one of feeling unable to keep still by her daughter's sickbed, the other from being nearly killed by horses out of control. These two grave frights were subsequently associated to any later fright and 'were eventually linked up with so many traumas, had so much reason for being reproduced in memory, that they perpetually interrupted the patient's speech for no particular cause, in the manner of a meaningless tic'.[26] In thinking through the temporal relationship between the different sets of memories, and how they link up to traumatic effect, Freud goes on to develop the concept of *nachträglichkeit*, or 'deferred action', whereby later events, even if trivial, serve to reawaken affect associated with earlier memories that had not been experienced as traumatic at the time, but which become so when being placed within a chain of related occurrences.

In the case of Frau Emmy, a complete cure was not immediately forthcoming. Freud explains this failure by asserting that the complete explanation could not be reached, and therefore the catharsis could not extend to the 'secondarily associated' traumas. He thereby reinforces the need for not leaving any gaps. In a footnote to this passage, Freud makes a clear plea for completeness and unprejudiced attention:

I may here be giving an impression of laying too much emphasis on the details of the symptoms and of becoming lost in an unnecessary maze of sign-

reading. But I have come to learn that the deter-
mination of hysterical symptoms does in fact
extend to their subtlest manifestations and that it is
difficult to attribute too much sense to them.[27]

In effect this forms the embryo of an alternate
system of joint narrative construction. It is an
endeavour which is only possible with patient and
therapist working in harmony. The patient's role
is to provide the tale (duly prompted by the therapist who elicits it from her) right down to its seemingly irrelevant details; irrelevant, that is, until he
provides the proper place for them in her story.

The case of Frau Emmy von N., in continuing to
elaborate the idea of the talking cure in this
manner, of necessity begins to tell the story of the
collaboration between patient and analyst. To be
sure, in this early account it took more the guise
of a struggle between the young Freud – anxious
about asserting his authority – and an aristocratic
wealthy patient, 'who clung so obstinately to her
symptoms', always insisting on being given good
reasons for giving them up; a patient who was fully
his match.[28] Underlying the demand for collabor-

ation, one can find the language of resistance, taken in both the military sense and in the emerging psychoanalytic sense. Freud's weapons were the same as those of Charcot and Bernheim: hypnosis and suggestion. He ordered, as well as listened and explained; he even went as far as to implant post-hypnotic orders in Frau Emmy, as if to convince them both of his ultimate authority and professional competence.

With subsequent cases, an ambivalently authoritarian Freud insisted upon investigating the genesis of individual symptoms. He no longer employed hypnosis as his ally when he took the case of Miss Lucy R., a young English governess who suffered from strange olfactory hallucinations. Lucy worked far from home for a wealthy and stern widower with small children, and her story sounds as though it could have been lifted straight from Gothic fiction. Freud's attempts at producing a trance had failed and he had to rely on the quality of his patient's reminiscences. This could only be achieved gradually and painstakingly, Freud leading his patient through three different levels of awareness as he took the

narrative to ever increasing stages of completeness. The avowed aim in this case lay 'in com-
pelling the psychical group that had been split off
to unite once more with the ego-consciousness'.[29]
It followed that the different psychic realms that
his patients inhabited were interrelated. Freud
invoked the precedent of Bernheim who had
already shown that 'the memories of events during
somnambulism are only *apparently* forgotten in
the waking state and could be reawakened by a
mild word of command'.[30]

Freud's role became more and more clearly
defined as one in which he would provoke reminiscences. This retrieval of memories would then
move the patient's narrative to ever greater degrees
of completeness. Freud as analyst enabled the
patient to remember and to share with him these
memories, despite her obvious reluctance. His
strategic interpretations functioned in the same
way as his suggestions had: they were his weapons
against the patients' resistances. However, they
also served as prompts for the patient's narrative,
moving it to another level, radically altering the
nature of the story, like a corner turned abruptly.

In the case of Miss Lucy, such a moment occurred when Freud suggested to her that she was in love with her employer. After that point 'she showed no resistance to throwing light on the origins of this inclination', which the patient had not previously indicated in any way. But a new olfactory hallucination – of cigar smoke, replacing the old one of burnt pudding – alerts Freud to the fact that the story is not complete. Freud relates the new smell to the employer's violent temper. And Freud did have the final say. Lucy had to contend with Freud's explanation: she loved her employer. She confirmed this readily, and answered Freud's question as to why she did not admit it previously with the paradox of knowing and not knowing:

I didn't know or rather I did not want to know. I wanted to drive it out of my head and not think it again; and I believe latterly I have succeeded.[31]

This was a perfect illustration of the psychoanalytic concept of denial.

Freud's service to the hysteric was not merely to

eliminate her symptoms, it was to allow her access to knowledge of her own desire, a desire felt to be in conflict not only with what was possible, but with what was socially permissible, indeed permissible to one's conception of one's self. In the final case in the volume, that of Elizabeth von R., the patient's hysterical symptom of debilitating pain in her legs is shown to have been caused by her inability to acknowledge the love she felt for her sister's husband and the thought she had at her sister's deathbed: 'now he can be mine'. It is within this dynamic of conflict that the psychoanalytic concept of repression emerges. Hysterical symptoms are caused by the contradiction between two impulses: a wanting which accepts no limits, and a desire to conform to the limits imposed by society. This will pave the way to the elaboration of what Freud saw as the cornerstone of his theory, the Oedipus complex. However, what was still implicit in his views on hysteria at that time, was that his method relied on uncovering actual traumatic occurrences in his patients' lives. At this stage, the talking cure was essentially a cure through catharsis.

Sexuality, seduction and the Oedipus complex

In 'History of the Psychoanalytic Movement' (1914), Freud remembers how three of his teachers – Charcot, Breuer, and the Viennese gynaecologist Rudolf Chrobak – put a conception of a problematic sexuality (where desire comes into contradiction with an incapacity to find fulfilment) at the very heart of their views on neurosis generally and hysteria in particular. Charcot had reputedly told him, in an excitable tone of voice, how in such cases it was always '*la chose génitale*— the genital thing'. Chrobak, when faced with a patient still a virgin after eighteen years of marriage, reputedly had said that the only prescription that would do her any good was one he could not write: '*penis normalis, dosim, repetitur*'.[32] But let's translate. 'All she needs is a good fuck', is what they are all, in fact, saying. Some women might well agree, but in others such sentiment would, in itself, be enough to provoke a hysterical fit of anger or laughter. A woman needs a man like a fish needs a bicycle?

A woman's voracious sexuality has indeed long

been part of the many discourses surrounding hysteria. But for Freud, this was no longer a matter of explicit or implicit moral condemnation, with scabrous undertones. It was simply part of his elaboration of the effects of psychic conflict. As such it would need to be of universal applicability, relevant to men as well, relevant to himself. One early lesson, crucial to the basic philosophy of psychoanalysis ('Know Thyself') had to be learned, and it had to do with the issue of 'owning up to desire' – and in this, both doctor and patient are implicated. A related point, and Breuer's experience bore this out, had to do with the acknowledgement and use of the phenomenon of *transference*. Distinct from Bernheim's technique of suggestion, which highlighted the commands given to patients, transference placed the therapeutic relationship at the centre of cure, and simultaneously displaced it from the here and now. The analyst becomes a stand-in for important figures from patients' pasts; in the case of Anna O., presumably, the sick father she had been nursing. Transference thus functions as the counterpoint to the Oedipus complex: according to psychoanalysis, the universal phenomenon of the child's love and hatred for its progenitors.

When Freud started specialising in the treatment of hysterical patients, case after case pointed to a *single cause* as the origin of the trauma: incidents of being sexually abused in childhood, most often by a member of one's own family, frequently the father. Freud thought that he had found a foolproof way of explaining neurosis, until he came up against what he saw as a flaw in his explanation: the sheer number of instances of such 'seductions' being reported to him. Too many cases defied common sense. 'Seduction' could not stand in his eyes as a general explanation for neurosis, for he could not believe that all neurotics had been 'seduced'. This forced him to seek the key to neurotic phenomena somewhere else. He shifted the causation of the trauma from an external factor, to an internal one: the hysteric's own fantasy life, her own desires, would hold the basic solution to the puzzle of reminiscence, and this could carry a truly universal applicability, valid for everyone, whether neurotic or not, whether patient or physician:

A single idea of general value dawned on me. I have found, in my case too, [the phenomenon of] being in love with my mother and jealous of my father, and I now consider it a universal event of early childhood.[33]

In effect, he had found his solution for the general workings of the human psyche in the Oedipus complex. In his next and most famous case study, 'Fragment of an Analysis of a Case of Hysteria', or the Dora case, Freud would attempt to deploy it relentlessly.

Dora, Freud and the unruliness of desire

Dora was the pseudonym for a young woman of eighteen who had been sent to see Freud by her father, after having threatened suicide. She had been suffering for some time from a series of relatively mild hysterical symptoms and was generally behaving in an intractable manner at home. The trouble-making that most upset her father concerned the accusations that his daughter was making against him and close friends of the family; a couple, identified as 'the K.s' in Freud's text. Dora maintained that her father was having an affair with the other man's wife, and that in order to buy the complaisance of the husband, he was quite willing to turn a blind eye to the fact that Herr K. was overtly propositioning his young daughter. Instead of making the angry Dora 'see reason', Freud, to his great credit, stated from the outset that he believed the complex amorous games she was describing. However, he put his own twist on it. He encouraged Dora to examine her personal active involvement in the story – that is to say, to look at her own desire. Unfortunately, he also had his own fixed idea as to which path that desire should and did take: in terms of Oedipal logic it would involve the father, and his stand-ins, namely Herr K. Her hysterical symptoms were no longer seen as a result of psychic trauma, but specifically in terms of Dora's conflicts around her acknowledgement and pro-cessing of what she (within these delimited terms) wanted.

The Dora case can be seen as bearing the mark of Freud's ambivalence about his new role as 'inventor of psychoanalysis': the text was a forum where his insights into the human psyche could be systematised and transmitted. His patients' knowledge now carried a different, more strategic usefulness. His own therapeutic role, as a result, became more urgent and forceful, without, however, silencing his patient completely. As part of his narrative of the case, Freud depicts Dora's 'resistance' to his interpretations, with a real sense of annoyance. He accuses her of 'playing secrets', dismisses her persistent claims that she did not find Herr K. attractive, and so on.

Yet, still, Freud does not deny Dora a voice. He might make it clear that 'the doctor knows best' with a high-handedness worthy of Charcot ('a no means yes, and a yes means yes', he notoriously affirmed); however, the structure that Freud adopted for organising his account of the story of the treatment was self-consciously fragmented. This was signalled by the official title 'Fragment of an Analysis of a Case of Hysteria', and by a lengthy discussion in the preface of the fragmentary nature of the hysterical narrative itself, in which he compares it to:

an unnavigable river whose stream is at one moment choked by masses of rock and at another divided and lost among shallows and sandbanks.[34]

It is only in the last telling, after much analytic work, that such a narrative would yield an 'intelligible, consistent and unbroken case history'.[35] Dora's story would never come to that – she broke off the treatment – but there was also something in Freud's understanding of their interaction which precludes the completion of the story. In this respect, it is significant that, as Toril Moi puts it:

Freud's text oscillates endlessly between his desire for complete insight or knowledge and an unconscious realisation (or fear) of the fragmentary, deferring status of knowledge itself.[36]

Inasmuch as Dora breaks off the treatment and refuses to grant Freud confirmation of what he maintains to be *his* knowledge of *her* desire (be it for Herr K., her father or her analyst), she allows him the space – both in his narrative as well as in his theory – to be taught by her. The psychoanalytic knowledge that Freud finally gains from Dora, albeit reluctantly and in a limited way, concerns the labile and endlessly surprising nature of desire itself. Two footnotes towards the end undermine – or, at the very least, immensely complicate – the entire edifice of his text, from both a theoretical and a narrative point of view. In these footnotes, Freud admits that he had overlooked the 'strongest unconscious current in [Dora's] mental life': her love for Frau K.[37] Subsequent critics of the case, starting with Jacques Lacan, point to the glaring fact that Freud, for all his urging Dora to own up to her desire, was tripped up by not knowing his own. Identifying with the virile Herr K., he ignores his own counter-transference arising from the analyst's involvements and identifications, and therefore misreads Dora's.[38] He does not heed the lesson that the hysteric tries to teach him; namely, the unruliness of desire. What the readers of Dora's case history find a century later, however, is not the story of a budding lesbian, but rather that of a young woman with many different identifications and desires. She strives to possess the men *and* the women in her life, she wants to be like them *and* as unlike them as possible. Dora – or Ida Bauer, as she was actually called – subsequently married, but kept in touch with Frau K. (Frau Zellenka). The two of them teamed up to become bridge instructors in Vienna in the 1930s.[39]

Hysteria, feminism and psychoanalysis

The case of Dora served as a powerful rallying point for feminist critics of the 1970s who were taking Freud and psychoanalytic theory to task for functioning within patriarchal assumptions that silenced women, forced them into modes of behaviour or thought which were detrimental to them, taking for granted certain assumptions about the way one assumed masculinity and femininity within society; assumptions which privileged the former over the latter. The trouble with Dora, the trouble with hysterics, was that they just did not conform.[40]

Interestingly, the link between woman's dissatisfaction with her lot and hysteria was clearly drawn in late 19th-century/early 20th-century discourse. On the one hand, pamphlets were circulated seeking to discredit suffragettes with accusations of hysteria, for example. On the other hand, Freud and Breuer's case studies point out that their patients were all intelligent women frustrated in their intellectual abilities. Georgette Dega, one of the first women in Europe to study medicine, trained at the Salpêtrière, and came to much the same conclusion, some time earlier, when observing Charcot's hysterics.[41]

The charge of hysteria was double-edged: as a hysteric, one was seen as either conforming too well, or else rejecting traditional models of femininity. The suffragette clearly belonged to the second type. What of the women performing for Charcot at the Salpêtrière? What of actresses, *demi-mondaines* and even respectable countesses retiring with 'shattered nerves' into darkened bedrooms? Twentieth-century feminists took up the issue by asking, 'Is hysteria a positive or a negative reaction to oppressive and frustrating social realities'? That is to say, is the hysteric a rebel or a victim? A first wave of scholarship, born out of a union of anti-psychiatry and feminism, looked back at the entire history of the disease in terms of a concerted effort on the part of doctors and priests to understand, control and if that failed, to discredit women. Hysteria's symptoms were bodily manifestations of the complaints of women who were denied a voice. However, the story gets somewhat more complicated by a closer look at these women's lives.

Scholars turned their attention to the true identity of Anna O., Bertha Pappenheim. Though by no means immediately cured by Breuer's intervention, she became a pioneering figure of the German women's movement, dedicating her life to a variety of causes involving women's welfare. Could hysteria be a source of empowerment rather than a handicap? 'Anna O.' channelled what ailed her into a socially transformative activity. In this model, hysteria becomes the flip side of feminism rather than the result of patriarchal oppression. But it is important to remember that in Bertha Pappenheim's case, hysterical illness and feminist activism did not coincide. Rather, she needed to work through the former to reach the latter. They were born out of the same unease but represented different courses of action. [42]

Of all these late 19th-century patients, it was the figure of Dora that crystallised the feminist imagination, becoming a figure of admiration for many. Her battle of wills with Freud, her adolescent stubbornness and selfishness, and her final partial triumph in leaving treatment served as an inspiration to feminist writers. Dora as heroine? But it is as insufficient to praise the hysteric for resisting the controlling interpretations of her doctors, as it is to pity her as their silenced victim. Rather, it is more fruitful to look at the *ambiguity* of the hysteric's position. Her sick role involves a passive resistance and definite suffering, whilst it affords her a new kind of gravitas within the household. As Carroll Smith-Rosenberg explained in a groundbreaking paper on 19th-century nervous disorders amongst the wealthy in New England:

No longer did she devote herself to the needs of others, acting as self-sacrificing wife, mother, or daughter: through her hysteria she could and in fact did force others to assume those functions [. . .].

Through her illness, the bedridden woman came to dominate her family to an extent that would have been considered inappropriate – indeed, shrewish – in a healthy woman.[43]

In other words, hysteria manifested itself as *both* a pathological effect of patriarchy and its subversion. A (for the most part, unconscious) complicity existed between doctors – who were paid to watch over hysterical women confined in bourgeois households – and their patients, whose condition was both the result and the way out of the intolerable conflicts and limitations of their lives. For every Bertha Pappenheim who managed to find a way to transcend the paradox, there were many others who could not. But, arguably, Bertha-the-feminist was no longer Bertha-the-hysteric. She was a chaste, staid, serious, intensely committed woman who founded orphanages, combated prostitution and fought against the abuse of alcohol. But some of us might feel, as the writer Patricia Dunker does, that what is also needed is to put 'the sex back into sexual politics and the camp back into campaigning'.[44]

For the feminist lessons of hysteria itself, we must look elsewhere, perhaps, to the contradictory aspects of the doctor–patient relationships which framed it in the late 19th century. Let us recall the eroticised spectacles of the Salpêtrière. The star performers undeniably profited from giving the doctors what they wanted: they gained attention, notoriety, better treatment. It is, in fact, the spirited exchanges of the young Ida Bauer with her physician that have inspired so many subsequent writers. Dora and Freud each had something the other needed. She was neither victim nor heroine, and he was neither villain nor selfless physician – or perhaps they were each a little bit of both. The theoretical lessons that psychoanalysis draws from hysteria involve precisely this *contradictoriness* of hysteria. The hysteric, according to the terms set by Freud, is the one whose fantasies do not allow her to choose between being a boy or a girl. She and/or he is the one who is always wanting but refuses the responsibilities or the consequences of this wanting – she and/or he wants but refuses to have. And what is it that in terms of psychoanalytic theory is the ultimate possession? Well, the penis, of course: phallic power. And it is precisely phallic power, which motivates and cements patriarchy, that the hysteric both wants and rejects. And it is in this that rests both the hysteric's plight and her/his potential subversiveness.

The perils of masculinity

But what of men then? According to psychoanalysis, they stand, it would appear, in a different relation of identification to social laws than women. After all, these laws – which rely on the threat of castration and a submission to a superego based on a fantasy of an all-powerful father – would seem to concern them more directly than women. That is to say, within these psychosocial arrangements, men have *everything* to lose: their penises (women, we are told, are already castrated) and their status (the son who bows to paternal injunction does so with the understanding that he too could be a father one day, but the daughter has no such option). In fact, the controversial question of male hysteria was an important aspect of the 19th-century discourse on the disease. For example, it was one of Charcot's pet interests: he needed it to strengthen the case he was making for hysteria's root in the nervous system. Accordingly, his descriptions of the attacks of male patients at the Salpêtrière conform to the same pattern as those of his female ones. However, it was not simply severing the link between hysteria and the female body which was at stake. Hysteria, as we have seen earlier, had become synonymous with excesses in female behavioural tendencies.

To account for the potential susceptibility of men to hysteria, two main explanatory schemes were used in 19th-century discourse. Men, as opposed to women, tended to become ill through an actual physical shock and not a psychic one. For example, strapping workers fell victim to industrial accidents, and although their injuries proved physically superficial they found themselves completely incapacitated. The alternative explanatory scheme was to de-masculinise the patients, to see them as men who were not quite 'real men'. So potential victims would be described as effeminate, or as belonging to certain 'suspect' racial groups such as Jews or Arabs. The language of hereditary taints and medical pathology would come into play here. Moreover, some of these men were exemplary of a type which was just emerging within medical discourses. According to Michel Foucault's famous thesis in *The History of Sexuality*, Volume 1 (1976), it was then that:

the psychological, psychiatric, medical category of homosexuality was constituted [. . .] less by a type of sexual relations than by a certain quality of sexual sensibility, a certain way of inverting the masculine and the feminine in oneself.[45]

These qualities, the masculine and the feminine, are clearly not understood as absolute essential categories but as internalised ideals one is bound to either follow or resist. Hysteria becomes thus a male solution to the burden of masculinity, couched, however, in feminine associations. The woman is the original rebel, the one who has less to lose, because she has less.

In the first acknowledged category of male hysterics – the 'worker' – it is the obligations of strength, duty and continued performance under any circumstance, which cause the crises. It is precisely these masculine virtues which were called upon in abundance during the appalling conditions of trench warfare in the First World War. It was at that time that men suddenly became the most visible group of sufferers. Although the diagnosis of hysteria was available to them, doctors and journalists called the ailment 'shell-shock', in reference to the immediate physical shock of an exploding shell, which was identified as having caused its onset. This new name made it sound more respectable and credible. Just like hysteria in women, however, it involved strange bodily disturbances which seemed to be unrelated to actual physical injuries. As in the case of hysteria, the patient's trustworthiness was in question, although this was even more at stake in a situation of war. As it was, many victims found themselves accused of cowardice and faced summary court-martials and executions rather than hospitalisation. The response of army physicians was dictated by the situation at hand: their priority was to try to get the soldiers returned to the front, often using mechanical means such as electric shocks to do so. Some of these physicians, such as Freud's close friend, Sándor Ferenczi, were also trained in the emerging discipline of psycho-analysis. Explicitly linking the soldiers' ailments with a psychoanalytic understanding of hysteria, they were well aware that, here too, conflict was involved in the symptom. In his paper 'Two Types of War Neurosis' (1916), Ferenczi identified it as the soldiers' idea of themselves as men coming into conflict with the realities of situation. The most common symptoms, such as severe disturbances of gait, were aligned with a collapse of narcissistic defences and subsequent regression to infantile in-capacity. The soldiers toddled like small children.[46]

These theories are compatible with an under-standing of these men as profoundly at odds with the masculine virtues from which they gained their sense of self. Juliet Mitchell puts the injunction with which they were faced in the following way:

The task for men was clear: accept the law of the father and you will not be hysteric.[47]

As men, their Oedipal socialisation renders them

at the same time beholden to and identified with the principle of paternal rule. So in the face of intolerable violence, the scaffolding of masculinity collapses and is shown to be a masquerade. The alternative response is to embrace the notion of a certain kind of masculinity as untenable. While stereotypes of the 'hysterical queen' in our culture may well be born out of homophobia and speak of rigid views of how men and women should behave, the drag queen – just like the 19th-century female hysteric – can also be seen as the one who knows the sham of these constraints and subverts them in performing them to perfect excess.

Let us take the classic Hollywood comedy *Some Like it Hot* (1959). The two male leads, Jack Lemmon and Tony Curtis, take up the roles of musicians fleeing from the mob, and spend most of the film in drag, hiding out in the midst of an 'all-girl' band whose lead singer is played by Marilyn Monroe. What delicious irony: Lemmon and Curtis performing womanliness alongside the most famous performer of womanliness of them all! The final scene, however, bypasses Miss Monroe and is worth recalling here. Jack Lemmon's character, Daphne, is trying to fend off a very persistent millionaire, Osgood.

Daphne: [. . .] *I've got to level with you – we can't get married at all.*
Osgood: *Why not?*
Daphne: *In the first place I'm not a natural blonde.*
Osgood: *It doesn't matter.*
Daphne: *I smoke, I smoke all the time.*
Osgood: *I don't care.*
Daphne: *But I'm a girl with a past. For three years I've been living with a saxophone player.*
Osgood: *I forgive you.*
Daphne: *I can't have children.*
Osgood: *We can adopt some.*
Daphne: *You don't understand, Osgood . . . Oh, I'm a man!*
Osgood: *Well . . . nobody's perfect.*[48]

Now you see it, now you don't

The soldiers of the First World War were the last significant group of patients who suffered from hysteria. However, this was far from a straight-forward matter. Although some psychiatrists, particularly those versed in psychoanalysis, explicitly acknowledged the nature of their plight as a hysterical disorder, it was the name of shell-shock that stuck. In the course of the 20th century, the diagnosis of hysteria became virtually extinct. At the same time, though, the term continues very much to be used on a day-to-day level. Furthermore, academic interest, particularly in the humanities, has grown, reaching a peak in the last decade.

Although hysteria is still absent from psychiatric diagnostic manuals, there has been continued, albeit muted, interest for it within the profession. Two books dedicated to hysteria, by practising psychoanalysts Christopher Bollas and Juliet Mitchell, have recently been published. The former argues that hysteria never went away but has been swallowed up by the more general diagnosis of 'borderline personality disorder'. Bollas brings the hysteric back to life in the contemporary world by vividly portraying her in a wide range of clinical narratives based on his own analytic work, as well as the work of analysts he has supervised. And she (and often he) is a startlingly familiar figure, with a conflicted sexuality, seductiveness, withdrawal, yet accompanied by a compulsion to take the centre stage, as in this quotation taken from the self-description of a homosexual patient:

I would drive my lovers crazy, I mean really drive them mad. Because when I would pick them up, I would be in a spell of the erotic, really into being sexual, and . . . I was bait, boy was I bait. I got carried away by it, off on it. And a lover would take me off with him, but when we got to the place to fuck, something else overcame me . . . a sort of, well an odd feeling that I was also on the verge of sainthood.[49]

Hysteria could never disappear, Bollas argues, because it is a reaction to the emergence of sexual awareness in childhood; more precisely, to the parents' reaction (whether accepting or rejecting) to that emergence and to their child's body as potentially sexual. Sexuality – and its avatar, hysteria – transforms the child's hitherto secure place in the family, and its relations with its parents, and is applicable to both genders. It is, however, as in earlier eras, suffused with the burden of femininity.

Mitchell's thesis is quite different. She too states that hysteria is a potentially universal human reaction to conflict. However, unlike Bollas who writes following a line of argumentation which is to all intents and purposes Oedipal (focused on the triangular relationships of love and hate between the child and its parents), Mitchell's point is that Freud's Oedipal scenario in fact distracted from the conflicts involved in *sibling* relations. These are the child's first lateral social relations, and as such the source of hysterical distress. It is sibling relations that rupture the narcissism of 'his majesty the baby';[50] a hysteric (and by this logic we are all implicated) is someone who has come face-to-face with the intolerable fact of his or her expendability. No one is special, everyone can be replaced. Mitchell offers a broader social basis and applicability to hysteria amongst individuals and nations, allowing the death-drive, envy and aggression to take centre stage – placing violence within the brotherhood of man. She discusses, for example, how the pressures of war may cause hysterical paralysis in the conflicted soldier, but the conflict is also expressed in rape, an all-too-common occurrence. But it remains unclear whether there is a place for a creative, regenerative hysterical grievance.[51]

But why has hysteria gone underground in clinical discourse? According to the historian of medicine, Marc Micale, hysteria had extended itself to breaking point, become an over-generalised, all-encompassing diagnosis by the end of the 19th century, a kind of 'waste paper basket of medicine' in the words of a follower of Charcot. In the first decades of the 20th century, it simply splintered into different kinds of disorders, separate diagnoses relating to the now separated-out symptoms. For example, disturbances of appetite, which had been one of the more usual symptoms of hysteria, were now seen as 'new' disorders: anorexia, bulimia, compulsive eating. Likewise, multiple personality disorder could thus be interpreted as an offshoot of hysteria.[52]

Elaine Showalter also argues that certain inexplicable mass phenomena are our epoch's version of hysteria. She discusses six different modern 'hysterical epidemics': chronic fatigue syndrome, Gulf War syndrome, recovered memory, multiple personality syndrome, satanic ritual abuse and alien abduction. All these phenomena are connected through the distinct question mark placed upon the actual reality of certain afflictions which nevertheless are deeply felt by, and deeply disturbing to, the sufferers. She describes debates – about the trustworthiness of patients, the quest to probe the materiality of subjective forms of distress, the dynamics of proof and the charismatic nature of healing – which have startlingly familiar echoes in the contextualisation of hysteria and its treatment.[53] However, these modern ways of expressing distress and conflict have at their disposal the resources of the information age. As Klaus Theweleit points out:

these are transmitted epidemics, electronically broadcast epidemics organised by the media, causing certain 'hystorical' symptoms. Their common characteristic of being broadcasted is the mark of their reality – and a great advantage.[54]

Their rate of growth, spread and/or dismissal is quicker than in previous times. Hysteria, from a widespread if individual struggle, takes on the guise of social phenomena which may well be scoffed at and rejected by many, but will always find ways of forging alliances. What seems to have been lost, with these descriptions of the growth and splintering of hysteria, is the question as to whether it can still function as a mark of dissent.

Hysteria and consequences

Writing in the journal *La Révolution Surréaliste*, Louis Aragon and André Breton singled out hysteria as an exemplary human revolutionary activity:

Hysteria is a more or less irreducible mental state, characterised by a subversion of the relations established between the subject and the moral world, of which the hysteric subject believes itself to be practically relieved, outside all delirious systems. This mental state is founded on the need for a reciprocal seduction, which explains the hurriedly accepted miracles of medical suggestion (or countersuggestion). Hysteria is not a pathological phenomenon and can, in all respects, be considered to be a supreme mode of expression.[55]

The classic figure of the hysteric has a creative appeal that many artists have tapped into during the course of the last hundred years. There are multiform examples of this kind of engagement: from the Surrealists' glorification of Charcot's star performers in their pamphlets and poetry, to Mary Kelly's reworking of the Salpêtrière's iconography in terms of everyday objects in her 1984–5 work 'Corpus', to Louise Bourgeois's recreation of the famous hysterical fit in bronze using a model of a contorted male body in her 1993 sculpture 'Arc of Hysteria'. But is it a matter of a 'subversion of the moral world', as Aragon and Breton would have it?

Thinking about what our culture calls hysteria, some images/usages stand out for me. Significantly, they involve the dimension of a mass phenomenon; in other words, hysterical identifications whereby beliefs and modes of behaviour become shared amongst members of a group: your desire becomes my desire becomes his and his and hers. The first image that comes to mind is of screaming teenagers at a pop concert, faced with their idol in the flesh; whether involving The Beatles or Britney Spears, the 'mania' is the same.

And then I think of fans at a football match on the verge of violence, so easily veering from team spirit to ugly racism and back again. Or then again, crowds baying for the blood of convicted child-molesters, child-killers, or even killer children. In a second set of contemporary hysterias, I reflect on the notion of groups – associations of concerned citizens or legislators – seeking to ban or regulate something. The objects of their wrath vary widely: Marilyn Manson, the age of consent between homosexuals, drug use, the consumption of beef, the proliferation of nuclear weapons outside the safety of Western controls, etc. But now I notice something rather paradoxical: when groups of people are united through behaviours or positions in ways which may be called hysterical, hysteria actually loses its power of protest. It seems to function as an empty category. What is wanted or not wanted matters little: anything could potentially take up the place of desire. Could hysteria mean anything other than exaggeration, over-reaction, in this context? Silly or ineffectual at best, murderous at worst?

Hysteria, then, as its history shows, is best

understood as an *individual's* act of protest and rebellion directed *against* social conditions. All human beings, of all genders, are free to partake. Hysteria has its risks, but sooner or later, we all run them, or indeed run up against them. For better or worse.

As the session proceeded I was dominated by two completely different states of mind. On the one hand, I found her immensely appealing and deeply moving, and totally in need of help. On the other hand, she scared the hell out of me and I was wondering whatever I was going to do with her and who I can find to 'take her on'.[56]

I see you shiver with antici . . . pation
But maybe the rain is really to blame
So I'll remove the cause (ha ha ha)
But not the symptom.[57]

Notes

1. Sigmund Freud, 'Femininity', in *New Introductory Lectures on Psychoanalysis* (1932), in *The Standard Edition of the Complete Psychological Works of Sigmund Freud* (in 24 volumes, hereafter *SE*), trans. James Strachey, London: Hogarth Press, 1953–74, Vol. 20.

2. Freud, *The Interpretation of Dreams*, in *SE*, Vols 4/5, Chapter VII.

3. Hysteria has consistently been of theoretical interest to Lacanian psychoanalysis. See, for example: Monique David-Ménard, *Hysteria from Freud to Lacan*, trans. Catherine Porter, Ithaca, NY: Cornell University Press, 1989; Juan-David Nasio, *Hysteria from Freud to Lacan: The Splendid Child of Psychoanalysis*, trans. Susan Fairfield, New York: Other Press, 1998. Recent books on hysteria by analysts of the British School will be discussed later on.

4. See: Marc Micale, *Approaching Hysteria: Disease and its Interpretations*, Princeton, NJ: Princeton University Press, 1995; Etienne Trillat, *Histoire de l'hystérie*, Paris: Senghers, 1986; Ilza Veith, *Hysteria: the History of a Disease*, Chicago: Chicago University Press, 1965.

5. Plato, *Timaeus*, in Edith Cameron and Huntington Cairns (eds), 'Plato: Collected Dialogues', trans. Benjamin Jowett, Princeton, NJ: Princeton University Press, 1978, p. 1210.

6. On heredity in 19th-century medical and social discourse, see: Jean Borie, *Mythologies de l'hérédité au 19e s.*, Paris: Galilée, 1981; Daniel Pick, *Faces of Degeneration: a European Disorder, 1848–1918*, Cambridge: Cambridge University Press, 1989.

7. For the background to mesmerism, see Leon Chertok and Raymond de Saussure, *La Naissance du psychanalyste de Mesmer à Freud*, Paris: Payot, 1973; Robert Darnton, *Mesmerism and the End of the Enlightenment in France*, Cambridge, MA: Harvard University Press, 1968; Alison Winter, *Mesmerized: Powers of Mind in Victorian England*, Chicago: Chicago University Press, 1998.

8. Jean Martin Charcot, *Leçons du Mardi faites à la Salpêtrière. Policlinique 1887–1888*, Paris: Progrès médical, Delahaye and Lecrosnier, 1888, pp. 100–101.

9. Georges Didi-Huberman, *Invention de l'Hystérie: Iconographie photographique de la Salpêtrière*, Paris: Macula, 1982.

10. Charcot, *Leçons sur les maladies du système nerveux faites à la Salpêtrière*, 3 volumes, Paris: Progrès médical, 1872–87, Vol. 1, p. 303.

11. Ruth Harris, 'Introduction' to Charcot, *Clinical Lectures of Diseases of the Nervous System*, London: Routledge, 1991, pp. 9–68.

12. Hyppolite Bernheim, *De la suggestion et de ses*

applications à la thérapeutique, Paris: Douin, 1886, p. 145.

13. Ruth Harris, *Murders and Madness: Medicine, Law and Society in the Fin de Siècle*, Oxford: Clarendon Press, 1989.

14. Pierre Janet, *L'Etat mental des hystériques: les stigmates mentaux*, Paris: Rueff, 1892, p. 158.

15. Ibid., p. 159.

16. Charcot, *Clinique des maladies du système nerveux*, Paris: Alcan, 1892–3, Vol. 1, pp. 97–117.

17. Charcot, 1888, pp. 322–3.

18. Jules Liégeois, *De la suggestion et du somnambulisme dans leurs rapports avec la jurisprudence et la médecine légale*, Paris: Douin, 1889, esp. pp. 468–72.

19. Charcot, 1888, pp. 322–3.

20. Charcot, 1892, pp. 103–4.

21. Freud and Josef Breuer, *Studies in Hysteria* (1895), in *SE*, Vol. 2, p. 25.

22. See Peter Gay, *Freud: a Life for our Times*, London: Macmillan, 1989, p. 67.

23. Freud and Breuer, 1895, p. 7.

24. Ibid., p. 35.

25. Ibid., p. 49.

26. Ibid., p. 93.

27. Ibid.

28. Ibid., p. 99.

29. Ibid., p. 123.

30. Ibid., p. 109.

31. Ibid., p. 117.

32. Freud, 'History of the Psychoanalytic Movement' (1914), in *SE*, Vol. 14.

33. Freud, in Jeffrey Masson (ed.), *The Complete Letters of Sigmund Freud to Wilhelm Fliess*, Cambridge, MA: Harvard University Press, 1985, p. 272.

34. Freud, 'Fragment of an Analysis of a Case of Hysteria' (1905), in *SE*, Vol. 7, p. 16.

35. Ibid., p. 18.

36. Toril Moi, 'Representation and Patriarchy: Sexuality and Epistemology in Freud's Dora', in Charles Bernheimer and Claire Kahane (eds), *In Dora's Case: Freud – Hysteria – Feminism,* New York: Columbia University Press, 1982, p. 187.

37. Freud, in footnotes to *SE,* Vol. 7, p. 120. Freud's last case – 'A Case of Homosexuality in a Woman' (1920), in *SE,* Vol. 18, pp. 147–72 – returns, twenty years later, to this neglected ground. It is interesting to note the contrast in Freud's attitudes in these two cases (his interpretations are harsher, more urgent, in the Dora case, for example), but also the similarities: an obtuseness in the face of a woman's desire.

38. Jacques Lacan, 'Intervention on Transference' in Juliet Mitchell and Jacqueline Rose (eds), *Feminine Sexuality*, London: Macmillan, 1982, pp. 61–73.

39. Lisa Appignanesi and John Forrester, *Freud's*

Women, London: Weidenfeld and Nicolson, 1992, p. 167.

40. See: essays collected in Bernheimer and Kahane, 1982, op. cit.; Hélène Cixous and Catherine Clément, *The Newly Born Woman* (1975), trans. Betsy Wing, Manchester: Manchester University Press, 1986; Elaine Showalter, *The Female Malady: Women, Madness and English Culture, 1830–1980*, New York: Pantheon, 1985.

41. Elaine Showalter, *Hystories: Hysterical Epidemics and Modern Culture,* London: Picador, 1998, pp. 52–3.

42. For a feminist perspective on Anna O., see Diane Hunter, 'Hysteria, Psychoanalysis and Feminism: The Case of Anna O.', in *Feminist Studies* (1983), Vol. 9, pp. 465–88, and for a revisionist clinical one, Max Rosenbaum and Melvin Muroff (eds), *Anna O.: Fourteen Contemporary Reinterpretations*, London: Free Press, 1984.

43. Carroll Smith-Rosenberg, 'The Hysterical Woman: Sex Roles and Role Conflict in Nineteenth Century America', in *Disorderly Conduct: Visions of Gender in Victorian America*, Oxford: Oxford University Press, 1985, p. 208.

44. Patricia Dunker, 'Post-Gender: Jurassic Feminism Meets Queer Politics', in Martin McQuillan, Graeme MacDonald, Robin Purves and Stephen Thomson (eds),

Post-Theory: New Directions in Criticism, Edinburgh: Edinburgh University Press, 1999, p. 60.

45. Michel Foucault, *The History of Sexuality*, Vol. 1 (1976), trans. Robert Hurley, Harmondsworth: Penguin, 1990, p. 43.

46. Sándor Ferenczi, 'Two Types of War Neurosis', in Julia Borossa (ed.), *Sándor Ferenczi: Selected Writings*, Harmondsworth: Penguin, 1999 , pp. 129–46.

47. Juliet Mitchell, *Mad Men and Medusas*, London: Allen Lane, 2000, p. 52.

48. *Some Like it Hot* (1959), screenplay by Billy Wilder and I.A.L. Diamond, directed by Billy Wilder (USA).

49. Christopher Bollas, *Hysteria*, London: Routledge, 2000, p. 99.

50. Freud, 'On Narcissism: An Introduction' (1914), in *SE*, Vol. 14, p. 102.

51. Mitchell, 2000, op. cit.

52. Micale, 1995, op. cit.

53. Showalter, 1998, op. cit.

54. Klaus Theweleit, 'Forms of hysteria in the Age of Modern media: Ghost Carriers and Protagonists of Hysterical Epidemics', in Silvia Eiblmayr, Dirk Snauwaert, Ulrich Wilmes and Matthias Winzen (eds), *Hysterie, Korper, Technik in der Kunst des 20 jahrhunderts*, Munich: Octagon, 2000, pp. 189–90.

55. Cited in Elisabeth Bronfen, *The Knotted Subject:*

Hysteria and its Discontents, Princeton: Princeton University Press, 1998, p. 174.

56. Bollas, 2000, op. cit., p. 128.

57. 'Sweet Transvestites', from *The Rocky Horror Picture Show* (1975), music and lyrics by Richard O'Brien.

Further Reading

Appignanesi, Lisa and John Forrester, *Freud's Women*, London: Weidenfeld and Nicolson, 1992.

Bernheimer, Charles and Claire Kahane (eds), *In Dora's Case: Freud–Hysteria–Feminism*, New York: Columbia University Press, 1985.

Bronfen, Elisabeth, *The Knotted Subject: Hysteria and Its Discontents,* Princeton: Princeton University Press, 1998.

Bollas, Christopher, *Hysteria,* London: Routledge, 2000.

Butler, Judith, *Gender Trouble: Feminism and the Subversion of Identity*, London: Routledge, 1990.

Cixous, Hélène and Catherine Clément, *The Newly Born Woman* (1975), Minneapolis: University of Minnesota Press, 1986.

David-Ménard, Monique, *Hysteria from Freud to Lacan: Body and Language in Psychoanalysis* (1983), Ithaca: Cornell University Press, 1989.

Ellenberger, Henri, *The Discovery of the Unconscious* (1970), London: Fontana, 1994.

Evans, Martha Noel, *Fits and Starts: A Genealogy of Hysteria in Modern France*, Ithaca: Cornell University Press, 1991.

Foucault, Michel, *Madness and Civilisation: A History of Insanity in the Age of Reason* (1962), New York: Random House, 1965.

—— *The History of Sexuality*, Vol. 1 (1976), Harmondsworth: Penguin, 1990.

Freud, Sigmund and Josef Breuer, *Studies in Hysteria* (1895), in *The Standard Edition of the Complete Psychological Works of Sigmund Freud*, trans. James Strachey, London: Hogarth Press, 1953–74, Vol. 2.

Freud, Sigmund, 'Fragment of an Analysis of a Case of Hysteria' (1905), in *Standard Edition,* Vol. 7.

Gilman, Sander et al., *Hysteria Beyond Freud*, Berkeley: University of California Press, 1993.

Goldstein, Jan, *Console and Classify: the French Psychiatric Profession in the Nineteenth Century*, Cambridge: Cambridge University Press, 1987.

Micale, Marc, *Approaching Hysteria: Disease and its Interpretation,* Princeton: Princeton University Press, 1995.

Mitchell, Juliet and Jacqueline Rose (eds), *Feminine Sexuality,* London: Macmillan, 1982.

Mitchell, Juliet, *Mad Men and Medusas*, London: Allen Lane, 2000.

Showalter, Elaine, *The Female Malady: Women, Madness and English Culture*, New York: Pantheon, 1985.

—— *Hystories: Hysterical Epidemics and Modern Culture*, London: Picador, 1998.

Smith-Rosenberg, Carroll, *Disorderly Conduct: Visions of Gender in Victorian America*, New York: Knopf, 1985.